2013

2013

—— by ——

SANDRA MADDIX

authorHOUSE®

AuthorHouse™ UK
1663 Liberty Drive
Bloomington, IN 47403 USA
www.authorhouse.co.uk
Phone: 0800.197.4150

*This book is a work of non-fiction. Unless otherwise noted, the author
and the publisher make no explicit guarantees as to the accuracy of
the information contained in this book and in some cases, names
of people and places have been altered to protect their privacy*

Published by AuthorHouse 09/08/2015

ISBN: 978-1-5049-4329-1 (sc)
ISBN: 978-1-5049-4330-7 (e)

Print information available on the last page.

This book is printed on acid-free paper.

2013

HERE COMES A POETIC STORY
ON THE CONSEQUENTIAL DAYS
PRETAINING TO OUR LIVES IN 2013

YOU CAN RELATE AND VERBALISE
AS YOUR STORIES UNFOLDS OR AMALGAMATE
KEEP READING THE PAGES AND YOU WILL REALISE
A VERY DISCREET CHANGE OR ONE QUITE INDEED
STAGNATE

AS ONE LIFE UNFOLDS AND TEACHES US
THAT WHAT WE ALREADY HAVE ATTAINED IS
BASICALLY JUST THE SAME
AND SIMPLY NOT A SCORING GAME

BUT WE STILL STRIVE AND LUST FOR MORE
WE PAY THE PRICE, NO SHAME FOR WHAT'S IN STORE
CHANGE 2013 FOREVER, NOW IS THE TIME TO LIVE YOUR
LIFE

FOREVER   **By Sandra Maddix**

DEDICATION

This book is dedicated to all of my family and friends, especially to those I have found via social networking. Blessed to you all my allowing me into your life, even though over the internet, I still felt I found something that was lost and now gained.

I would especially love to express my esteem dedication to my son Ceaké who has always been a positive factor a long by my side in everything we have accomplished this year.

Last and not least, to all of the team at Chipamunka publishing, without whom this book would not be published. I offer them my sincere blessing and gratitude.

Sincerely and lovingly all Sandra

ABOUT THE AUTHOR

I have learnt that every person has to go through some form of learning curve and that with hard work, this can be achieved.

To discover your abilities and the fact the openness allows you to reflect your inner emotions; is in actual fact an awareness that is very difficult to compete with in this everyday life

.

In fact, this openness of myself and my family has made me more of the person I wanted to become and I hope that my book will instil these properties into yourself and allow you to realise that everything is possible.

As my mother would say, "There is no such word as can't"!

Thank you All
Happy 2014

CONTENTS

2013

January 1st 2013

Dreams

Sleeping, but conscious, dreams; my reality even in my
deep sleep, subconscious
Dark, eerie can't quite fathom the entity of the
Wholesomeness I want to see

What is that? Then I see the light, bright but then
cometh the darkness
Run, run, hide and go towards the light
No, it's too bright

I shun my eyes and face, what's happening?
It must be a dream? A mystical

I'm scared; I look to the right and left, no one,
But some think. Someone is there
I'm not alone, some think, someone is here!

I've got to get out and run there
Or I'm I safe, just remain still?
But this is just a dream, not reality? I wake up

Sweating in my bed I'm still here
Oh god, that mystical affair was ballistic
So surreal and scary, but I'm still here
And I don't want to go back there!

Dreams, why can't I sleep?
Why do I have these dreams?
What do they mean? So profound! Too deep!
Rest again? Toss and turn and go back to sleep, my dreams they are just TOO DEEP!

January 6th 2013

<u>REMEMBERANCE</u>

Do you remember the chairs and the windowsills?
Sitting down or resting, as you played protected, with
your friends?

Do you remember the days when I said I already ate
(lied) and you had dinner and ice cream?

Do you remember your sleepness nights?
When I had to run down the stairs and reassure you
that you were safe
Cos mummy was there! Of course you're alright!

Do you remember the fun we had and the laughs with
stupidity
That made us happy not sad! Even the lacerated foot
in the swimming pool
Oh what an idiot I must have been, oh what a complete
fool!

Yes, that's my Mum, Oh yes it is (giggle). Oh fudge,
let's give her a kiss

Do you remember the long days and early mornings
Watching the Simpsons, playing dominoes, going to
bed yawning?

No, but you do remember all of the other things that mama had nothing to do with, but made you sad! Shame on you girl that was not me being bad! I might be silly, but certainly not MAD!

February 2nd 2013

ANOTHER LIFE

Today is just another day
Snowing, unusual, as the sun shines illuminating
rays
My life feels joyous and I don't know why
Problematic yes, but I'm not shy

I wait intrepidly for a moment to occur
Because since this year has began, event after
event, still leads to a blur

My cleaner arrives and informs me of her life
Again I feel such joy and with embrace
I make an undetermined choice

No matter how my life goes
I will literally take it by the balls
Go ahead, be positive, take some deep breaths
Elevate, erect, so as not to ascertain any falls

Just take a short pause

Look at this way, exuberance, my name
No time to exude and be apparent, who is or is not
to blame

Just learn by your mistakes and mines in error
Your life is yours and mines I refuse to live in terror

As from this day and days to come
I'll look after me and my only son

My babies I love them and always will
My Mother, my brothers and even who? Bill?
Well everyone, what I'm trying to say
Is don't waste your life on waiting for pay day!

February 12th 2013-11-11

Differences

What definitive argument has anyone got on being different?
We are all unique individuals with what or who we are – self!

What makes us different and what makes everyone so scared of 'it'?
Can they tell you anything or just talk shit!

Being different is in everyone's nature
Just like beauty and the beast, it still comes back to race, class or culture

Rich and poor, tall or short
We are all the same, we do as taught!

But underneath it all we are just the same with all of our differences
It can be exasperating to even consider it, especially concentrating on all of the sciences

Isn't it sufficient to believe that being yourself is different
And without our differences there would be no one
No us or any need to be different, but just one single entity,
All the same, similar, acting like robot with no differences and no one to blame
Because we're just all the same!

February 14th 2013

Valentines

Valentine, Valentines, what should I do?
Bake a cake or go and make love?
Stir around and mix for a hour
Stop thinking dirty and have a shower

Valentines, Valentines, what should I do?
I know what you decided
And that will be easier for you
Cos if you get it wrong, then the cake I will bake
But if you get it right, then the love we will make

Oooh Valentines I forgot about the groove
Making love, how to move
Just stop thinking, don't tremor or shake
Just take time, make love for goodness sake!

February 15th 2013

AROUND

Do you believe in what goes around comes back around?
Well I do. You see all through my life
I have observed and ascertained whilst attempting to understand
The reasons for certain events and why they actually do happen
The occurrences, the consequences and then ultimately the repercussions
All lead you back to that first point before you began your stretch

You see through Life we all undergo a learning curve
But sometimes that curve can and almost likely will deviate in a different direction
From this direction, you now have a different task to master, which will then determine
Another action that will resolve in another task that will again lead you back
To your first action!

This learning curve affects our lives and the people around you
It will with almost certainty have developed learning and behavioural factors that again
Will affect our lives

Some may hide an say 'yeah, what is she going on about now'?

My answer would be, 'What goes around always come back around.

Full circle, 360 degrees and if you don't undo the wrongs in your past

Your learning curve will simply multiply through your useless life and generations to come.

Your learning curve, will become others as well as your own

Never reaching a destination, always being on your own

So with your life always take seriously, the smallest details

With the greatest speed, like a yacht sailing by with the simplest of ease

Cos what goes around always come back around and we don't want to start beginning at the start all of the time!

February 16th, 2013

D'accord

Okay, you come around with plenty to say
Today the same for you, like every other
What did the bull do to the brother?

You seemed 'pissed off'
You grunt and sigh, you almost look like you want
to cry
You turn your head and look at me, for sympathy,
to hear your plea

I stare at you, Oh not again, I really love him, he is
my friend
But every day what more can I say, this brother has
got to live a different way
He asked if for a break my house he may stay
I look at him and shake my head to indicate, nay!

It might sound harsh, but I know he can do better
To live a productive life, become education
Be able to read his own letter

Today, I observe the change in him
He smiles, he's proud of what he found within
You see, he found his karma, his inner peace
And with that love and love
No more police
No more sin!

February 20th 2013

ANONYMITY

Not known, someone, not known, no one
Who's whole or partially named, unknown, but
someone

How can they observe or have this inherent capability
to endure
Such an antecedent time, enjoy, not becoming a chore

To see something of beauty in many forms or one
Can open your eyes to an unity
Of what you will be, to mould in what you will become

No now, not known, through your work, Yourself
Beholden, no physical reward but a self-satisfying
emotion
That yields greatness, which is your wealth

Only you can with assistance, can sustain
Make it entire and whole
When you are gone, your work will remain

Anonymity, you're not, your work will prevail
To tell parts of your life, not all a fairy tale
Anonymity, you're not. You've lived without knowing
And through your work you accomplished
Without strife, without knowing
It came so naturally, a joy to do
Because it did not seem like work to you

A legacy you leave, without even knowing
Anonymity you are not but someone worth 'knowing'.

February 21st, 2013

<u>A Prayer</u>

The Lord my god is my Father in spirit, body and soul
He alone commands me and makes me feel whole
He is my reason for being and seeing all the obstacles I
have to bear
He is the only being that I do fear

The Lord, My Lord, Father, Creator, Most High
He talks to me all day and all night
And on these special, exclusive days, he's all I hear
Every day and every night

The Lord, My God, Father Most High
Somehow, I feel him always by my side
And I have nothing, not even something from him to
hide
I keep myself in 'check'. I try not to 'slide'

To play games with Him is practically a sin
To play games with him is totally a sin
To hold my head up high and say unto him
I', m here for a reason, To serve Father, Most High

February 23rd 2013

WALKING AWAY

You can't just walk out?
No explanations why!
Do you not feel obligated to inform the person why?

Do they deserve to know or do you feel that this
decision was inevitable
If that's the case, why not leave earlier
Don't eat all the goodness first and then leave the
vegetables!

Well I walked out and now I can breathe
My sleep becomes me
I feel very much at ease

One thing I have realised
I can look after me but not everyone I find I can please

I don't want a man to be on a lead
Neither do I want a man that I can appease
To me he might as well just be on a lease
So instead of waiting I might as well leave

You can just walk out as you walked in
Another chapter in your life
Is just about to begin
Our time together was brief, quite short
But it taught me a lesson
Of some sort

Never leave 'self' for somebody else
To determine your future will surely be uncertain
To wake and not know may always be
The day that will go, is something you will treasure
You may not even know

So yes remember this, you can walk out and leave
I may or may not miss you, another time in my life
I wouldn't have taken it with such an ease

February 24th, 2013

SKITTS/STUPID

What's dat?
It works when it wants to?
Skitts it called, my little sister

Made my life, a flipping misery
I changed it though with your insincerity

You are so full of 'shit' and all of dat!
We all know that
Because it is a fact

You, my dear, whoever you are
Don't come near me
But stay very far

I don't need or want you
Cos 'crosses' you are
You are a liability and I detest you for who you are

Stay away I said, stay far
Because if you don't
I'll fuck you up and start war. STUPID

March 2nd, 2013

Love Letters To A Prisoner

I found some letters
Letters to a prisoner
A work of fiction, it can't have been reality

Some supervision, I must implore
I keep on reading, more and more

These letter depict a person in pain
She can't understand or go through the strain

Of being in solitude and no one around
No person to talk to, no friend has she found

These letters she'd read
They must be misleading
It informs her of matters that are quite deceiving
No more can she read
As her eyes misty over
To know it's her life she's reading
These letters to a prisoner

Love letters to a prisoner
Who is kept secluded
From a love one, her family
Her man included

Reality it is, but she'll be maimed
Mentally and spiritually, the system is playing a game
They are attempting to make her insane
To believe that these letters to the prisoner
Is addressed to her with her name

She cries and holds her head down low
It's not real, it cannot be
They are playing games on me, my enemies, my foes

It's all but a dream
She'll wake up one day
This nightmare will end
No letters in hand, but man by her side
She goes back to sleep to awake for that day

March 2nd, 2013

Slavery Over The Waters

Free and then stolen
Chained and snatching at morsels of food to survive
Learning new languages, dialects and hand signs
To communicate in order to contrive
This situation they're in, man, woman and child

By now they know its slavery
All they know is that they have to survive
Their captors show no mercy
As they check the chained merchandise

This is not a work of fiction told by historians
But of a period of slavery
That enslaved Black people from the beginning of
history

As I said before, this is not a work of fiction from historians
That has been written or told
It is about Black people, captured and treated inhumanely by others
Whipped, raped isolated, violated, abused
Punished severely, sometimes to the point of Death is they didn't do as told!

Thousands, millions died for freedom on this
'Translantic Slave Trade
Thrown overboard, for greed and space, to rid of
disease
To increase the survival rate of slaves for purchase in
which they'll be paid

You see? more money, no pain for them, just gain
Less Negroes to sell, so what, less strain, less to sustain
The more they could keep healthy that's all would
remain

To tell this story in such a short space
It cannot even begin to inform you of this disgusting
time or state
Of human history and of what man can do
And remain untouched by what they know is wrong
and unjust or true!

March 4th, 2013

Consolidation

Talk to a bredda last week
About debts and consolidation
Him so convincing
I nearly went for the solution

But no e-sign for me, paper I rely on
Praise God, cause me ring dis morning
And no bredda is talking!

Sidekick cum pun phone
Bullshit 'im talking
Trying to reassure me
That is the truth the bredda was talking

Well when I added it up
I only owe something
With my lifestyle
I will never owe nothing!

Consolidation, a rip off, a con
Best be bankrupt and pay as you can

March 5th, 2013

NSPCC

Please tell me how can they exist
No help, just money donations
And nothing stops, just keeps going on
We need to learn to co-exist
Children are children
And parents we are meant to be
Then no more money donations

NSPCC and a load more
If they listened to their parents
They would know for sure

All I care about is my kids
And so it should be, no NSPCC
But when taken out of my hands
How can I know for sure what will be
Am I their Mother or the NSPCC?

Can anyone answer that question?
I've been asking since the 4th
The system I have no faith in
They are the ones that make our children treat us like
their mate!
I dream, I think and I do not like what I see
Because if I can't protect my kids by law
What else can there be?

I have the answer to all of you
My life I have lived
My kids, I'll die for
And what I have acquired I will leave and give
To my kids, who love me for them I live
No NSPCC for me, but someone else
But us as parents need be given that right
To enable us to instil morals, values and respect
In order for our children to grow right
Before they enter society and always want to fight!

March 11th, 2013

AWAKEN

I am not tired though my eyes weep
I know I should be tired but I cannot sleep

A pill I take, a bath I make
And in my clean, lovely bed I go to relax
Only to remain awake

I have a nightmare, I woke up
Staring wide eyed into the dark
Looking around, scared but still sharp

My dog is not barking, my cat no meow
So what is disturbing me, so I can't sleep

I keep on looking into the dark
Then suddenly I see dawn coming
And hear the birds as they chirp
Its morning, but I have not slept
I climb out of bed nearly falling
Routine I have to do
And as I move around my home
I crept silently watching, waiting for what
I don't know

Oh I am just tired, prang and really upset
What's keeping me awake?
What's making me stress?
A realisation has just hit me and it might just come true!
The reason for awakening means something 'new'.

March 12th, 2013

WONDERING

I AWAKE ON THIS GLORIOUS BEAUTIFUL MORNING
CAN'T REMEMBER TOO MANY OF MY DREAMS
I DRAW MY CURTAINS, SMILING, STILL YAWNING

OH BUT BRIGHT AWAKE, I SEE AND KNOW
WHAT CERTAINLY HAS TO BE DONE
AND OF BLESSED TO THE FATHER MOST HIGH
BY HIS WILL, IT IS TO WHOM I WILL STRETCH
TO ASK UPON AND THEN IT WILL BE DONE!

DON'T BE AFRAID, BUT FEEL ENLIGHTENED
BECAUSE ON THIS DAY YOUR LIFE
WILL LEAD A DIFFERENT PATH FOR YOU AND I
TO FOLLOW WITH LOVE AND GRACE AND
FULFILLMENT
GIVE UNTO YOUR HEART, SOUL, SPIRIT AND BODY
EVENTUALLY TO ASK FOR ATONEMENT

GOD BLESS US ALL AND BELIEVE IN HIM
TAKE CARE OF MOTHER NATURE AND RECEIVE
WITHIN

BLESS THOSE THAT HAVE NOT
AND GIVE UNTO THOSE THAT HAVE NOT
THINK AND PONDER ON ALL OF YOUR THOUGHTS
BELIEVE IN THE TURTH, ENEGISE FROM THE LAND
LOOK AT THE TRINKETS THAT YOU HAVE BOUGHT!

THINGS, OH SILLY THINGS
THAT WE BELIEVE BRINGS
ALL THAT WE DESIRE, I GIVE UNTO GOD
BECAUSE ALL THAT I REQUIRE I ALREADY HAVE
OBTAINED THROUGH MY LOVE FOR GOD!

March 14th, 2013

NEVER ALONE

God has his arms around me
He's standing here beside me
No, He will never leave me
No, I am not alone

Now that God has found me
I feel his love surround me
No longer does doubt confound me
Cos my God is all around me

And No, I'm not alone
Cos I have got his arms around me

March 16th, 2013

Today

A poem today or not!
A shake, rattle and roll or mop?
House is clean, tummy is full, I've done a lot
And know I turn to the laptop
To see and read their absolute (nah stop)!

It cheers me up to hear and read
Cos it makes me realise that I'm not alone
My life not shite but if it were so
Then who would care, my Babies, my Fam
I don't think so and if they do, I don't think so!

Today I look at rain, but blue skies
My shine quicken and gleam, skint and shine
The sky looks so simple, but holds so much
Can change in an instant like breakfast and lunch

It's moody, not clingy, gets bored
Keeps us guessing what will come next?

The sky encompasses everything I am and yet not!
I sit quite comfortably in my chair
I look around me and I don't care
The world out there I don't not fear
Cos I know inside my God is near
I hold so dear, so nothing to fear!

March 17th, 2013

Slow, temperately, I move in y surrounding
My legs and feet hardly moving
Not making a sound
Sincerely, not allowing to cough or the music to
pound
To awake anyone, so I don't make a sound

The cat out lives my expectations, (meow, meow
etc....)
The dog then barks and then she hounds

Oh My God, there goes the Rabbits
The Lord's name I don't call in vain!
Trust me no doubt!

They're up! Hello in their own, distinctive way
Letting me know it's time to eat
And it's also, time too play!

I get back up and look around
Like a robot, I do my chores in a bound
Not twisting around

Let off the lead, clean up the mess, let the cat outside
And then she meows again
But then I rest and just pretend
I'll get back tom re-continue and then it's done

Believing I'm gonna get some
Both can't mistake the feeling of me
Nobody come again!

I turn my radio onto my favourite channel/DJ
That I appear to be into

Peace, One love, food is cooking
And MY daily chores are finished
Out the window I am looking

Yeah, too right, Nobody I am booking
My Life look too BRIGHT
FIRST IN A LONG TIME

SX

<u>UNCONDITIONAL LOVE!!!!!!</u>

Sublime, refine, sympathetic and kind
Joy, happiness, empathy, all unique
All that negativity, everyone leave
Left behind

Peeps, don't understand me, they really think they do!
I chat, I think pure nonsense
C os that's all I think they really think of 'YOU'

I say it in that way, in the 3rd person, I am
The second has gone, astray and the first is staying strong!

Don't, Shy? Outside, but get inside!
Your, Inspiration, goals and ambitions
For some reason, I feel I truly must hide!

Why I don't even know and to be honest
I don't want to, I just don't care
Sympathetic, honest, caring, bearing all of these qualities
They're mines, all mines!!!!!!!
I have NOTHING LEFT TO SHARE
FOR ME I CARE
MY CHILDREN WITH THEIR SIBLINGS I SHARE
NO PROBLEMS ANYWHERE
I AM STILL HERE WITH ALL THE CRAP

I AM MAMA AND PAP
RAPPA TAP I WAKE LIKE A BAGEL TO THE BAP
READY FOR THE ATTACK

I AM SO LUCKY THAT NOW I CAN RELAX
BLESSED YOU
JOY AND WISDOM TO THE WORLD. Xxx

SympATHETIC, HoNEST, Caring and all of ABOVE
AND THESE QUALITIES,
THEY'RE ALL MINES
AND I HAVE NUFF TO SHARE!!!!!!!!!!!!!1
BUT PLEASE BEWARE, I AM A MADDIX
SO DEFINE THAT WORD SHARE TO MEAN CARE!

THAT'S ALL I GOTTA SAY. NITE, NITE!
TO YOU MEN, DON'T LET THE BED BUGS BITE!
I'M SURE MAMA RAPPED YOU UP ALL SWEET AND
TIGHT!
GOODNIGHT!!!!!!!!

LOL. SX

Strategy

Suggest, ideals, moral and values
Sometimes, it's easier to compose

To verbalise, 'verbatim; one to oooone!
Can then suggest another reaction
Will propose/oppose!

Opposition can cause such a oblique suggestion
And gain quite a negative reaction
That one has already suppose
So to neutralise this insignificant situation
Let's give them an ultimatum

So compose, oppose suppose and definitely impose
And then finally, YOU explode into their reality
Trust, they will PROPOSE!!!!!!!

March 23rd, 2013

SEEING

My dreams mysterious and wayward bound
They take me an ancestral age of once a Queen
And then a Slave!

A martyr, upon to some and those I gave
My life meticulous and up and down
I move around without a sound

Life it seems, appear profound
So visionary, I see; my dream into the light
I drop off only for its return
Reminding me of life when it was safe and oh so sure!

Mistakes I've made, but no regrets
My dreams, clarity can quantify the lot
Today, the next, if blessed to come
I'll restrain my emotions and feeling to stand
To show, complain, compress my thoughts
My dream, you see, is all I have
Besides my Kids, I didn't bought, but I got the LOT!

Methodical, uncomplicated, but marginally close
I see the truth in dreamland, awake, yes both
They cometh together, but yet a gap remains
That gap whence breeched will be always is my
domain

Self on self, together intertwined
Dreamland and reality forever now true and mine

March 24th, 2013

OK BABES

HERE WE GO AGAIN?

HOW DOES SOMEONE LIKE ME, LOUD AND BOLD
LEARN TO TURN THE OTHER CHEEK?

I CLEAN, I COOK, I WASH EVERYTHING
SO BRILLIANT TO LOOK AT SO WHAT!
I'VE ACCOMPLISHED IN ONE MAGNIFIQUE
MOMENT
THAT BRILLIANT, ULTIMATE TOUCH, SO WHAT!

MY INNER SELF, BEYOND CONTROL, STAYS FOCUS
I JUST DON'T KNOW OR UNDERSTAND
THE WILL POWER I BEHOLD
I JUST CAN'T DO AS TOLD!

I'VE ACHIEVED BEYOND EXPECTATIONS
SOME SAY SUSS, BUT STAY AWAY FROM
SO I CAN'T FULFILL MY INTENTIONS

THEY DO NOT KNOW MY LIMITATIONS
YOU SEE A LOT OF PERSONALITIES
I HAVE TO EXPRESS TO SUBDUE MY COMPLICATIONS

NO ONE OVER, I DON'T EXPECT
TO UNDERSTAND MY PERSONANE
I STAND THEREFORE ERECT!

YOU SEE ME AS A ROBOT COS
THAT'S WHAT I PROJECT
BUT THE INNER ME A SECERT
THAT TO ME I DO PROTECT

NO ONE SEES FRAGILE I STRONG
NOT WEAK THEY LOOK UPON
BODY AND NO WRONG OR MEEK

I STAND TALL AND LOOK AT THEM,
I KNOW I'M NOT/AM WEAK BUT
YES I PRETEND.

TO SHOW YOU MY LACK OF ABILITY
IS AN EVENT I WONT A EXTEND
TO AFFILIATE, TO BE ME YOU WILL
COMPREHEND.

MY BODY, SPIRIT AND SOUL,
NEVER BEEN SAID UNTO MAN.

YOU SEE MY DANGERS
I COME FROM THE CREATOR
GOD AND IN THIS STAFF OF
HIS I WILL ALWAYS BE STRONG.

NO MORE LIABITIES TO HIM
MOST HIGH FATHER I BELONG.

WHAT DOES YOUR FUTURE HOLD IMAGINE?

SOME OF YOU ALL NEED TO GO
SOME MAY STAY, STAGNATED
AND QUITE UNDETERMINED OF THEIR
DESTINY AND THEN BE OBILERATED!

BUT BACK TO THE FUTURE IS WHERE I WILL
ALWAYS REMAIN
I AM NOT IN CAPTIVITY, MY FUTURE UNSTAINED

ALL I WANT FOR ONE AND ALL
IS TO ACHIEVE AND FEEL NO PAIN
AND WISHES TO COME TURE

GO FOR YOUR AMBITIONS AND WISHES TO
COME TRUE WITHOUT NO STRAIN
OH I FORGOT, NO POWER, NO PAIN

IT'S HARD OUT THERE AND PROBABLY WILL
GET HARDER OR NOT?
BUT WITH ALL YOUR HARD WORK
THE RESULTS WILL BE REWARDING, A LOT!
WHETHER YOU LIKE IT OR NOT!
THEN AGAIN, SAYING ALL THAT
IT COULD BE A LOT!

SO GO BACK INTO THE FUTURE
WHERE YOUR DESTINY AWAITS
AS ANEW, DAY COMES NEARER/CLOSER
AND EASIER WITHOUT REMINESCENCE OF THE
PAIN OR STRAIN!

THE PRESENT, THE PAST AND THE FUTURE
ARE ALL PART OF THE DAY
LOOK AGAIN INTO THE FUTUTRE
YOU'RE LIVING IT NOW
WHAT MORE CAN I SAY?

THIS WHOLE MEANGERIE OF BEING
DON'T MAKE MY DAY
BUT ONE MINUTE AGO IT WAS AND I KNOW
OVERS BUT ONES STILL HERE TO STAY

FULFILL MY DESYINY, LEAVE BEHIND A LEGACY
SOMEONE WHO'S LIFE I HAVE AFFECTED
AND CAUSED THEM TO BE EFFECTIVE

TODAY, TOMORROW, RIGHT NOW OR YESTERDAY
EVERYDAY, EVERYTIME IS JUST ANOTHER DAY
WHAT MORE CAN I SAY!
WE WILL GO FORWARD FROM TODAY.

Sx

MARCH, 2013

ENTRIES/JOBS

You know work
I mean real hard work, labour
It's not an easy job to do

You feel the pains, certain muscle dormant
Now come alive
No longer a learner, a worker, no student

You look around and up and above
No one's there, no one's love
But that I believe is what keeps you going
Knowing all the above, doing, not showing

You do and continue, so until your bodily being
aches
It so cold out there, so warm in here
But you won't stop until it's done!
Even when you're tired and you begin to shake!

Can you? Yes!
Will you? Yes!
Until your body says no, but you go on
Until that job is done!

You admire your work, half appreciating
Please no one don't ask to sit on my frustration
Deliberation with no satisfaction
Everyone looks, orate, but with no action

Tomorrow I'll continue and finish the job
I'll start again until completion
Keeping the mind and consciousness going
Today it done, looking good
No bad comments and no commotion

Get my wages, money in pocket
Pay my bills and after what government dock it
But I am happy, it's honest pay
My job I do this every day!

April 6th, 2013

Togetherness

Relationships, I believe is a partnership
Knowing, understanding, more than coping with it

Relationships can become stagnated
But just like life it can be evaluated

It can evolve into something meaningful
Or remain as nothing, if untruthful

Relationships, the ones that count!
Can make one feel invincible
Energised and beautiful

Now if relationships are of a negative form
Downfalls, basically nothing conforms

Put a halt, don't go no further
Because then it becomes onerous
And battles will follow
As I said put a halt to it and don't go no further!

April 9th, 2013

Relationships

Boyfriends, they come and go
They want their freedom, OH, NO NO NO!

They do want and need
What they want to do and everything depends on
YOU!

But trust me a 'boyfriend' is a single MAN
He is not your Husband, a free agent
Reasoning, obviously he don't understand

A Man you must have, to depend on and be with
To overs all of your situations and help to relieve it
So don't settle for less, than the man that you want
So a 'boyfriend' is just that and just wah hunt!

Do you really need it!!!!!!!!!!!!!!!
Sx

April 11th, 2013

HUMBLE PIE

Your Highness, Your Highness
How low do I bow and spread my arms around your
glorious embrace

Beauty, as they say, 'Is in the eye of the beholder'
But it's your backbone, this water, air and earth
That makes you more than that
But my head for your shoulder

Gracious, brilliant and splendour, beyond belief
Why do people destroy for monetary gain!
And want, not need and cause such grief
A long with such tremendous pain!

Oh how I love thee
To be in your presence day and night
For You! to honour Me, I hasten up to Thee
My Beloved, My Highness, My Gracious most beautiful
Mother Earth
Sx

MY LIFE

Today is full of crosses
Nothing, but everything I do or talk about
Gives me no gain, but losses

Today, I remonstrate, my life I live
I do protest, detest, to end this continuum of
absolute crosses

Today, I reprove my responsibilities and the regrets
that I had 'make'
But thinking, doing it was just for that moment, for
God's sake!

Today is not another day. I do now remonstrate
In all my actions, positive, I demonstrate
Today if 'fuckries', believe is deliberate

Not to conciliate or conclude these negative actions
But to approve and remove those negative actions

On higher planes I fly, not as a human
Pleased today Not!
But pleased today I am a Man
God has approved me; I receive the Lot!

April 16th, 2013

Cares and Fears

What is somebody when you feel like nobody?
Trashing through, pilfering, begging
To the same who are, what caring?

What is somebody? It could be me
Possibly you or nobody or do you care?

Well to put it straight
Somebody I am, nobody I am not
And anybody can believe somewhat!

It depends on what I'm dealing with
Are you worth it or not?
Cos this somebody here is worth alot!

That's somebody, no me and no but
I am nobody, but everybody, I am the lot!

Somebody please smile, give me a hug
Receptive I feel and quite smug

What is somebody, somebody like me?
Looking, observing and shining through
Not waiting, don't mistake it's probably not you
That somebody who's calling is God and that's true!

Who Cares

Resolutions, evolve solutions
But do they adjust?
To make you equate you must have some trust

Mines is less, I count on fingers
I do mean literally, not 'fishfingers', (lol)
Beefburgers, veggies, here we go
I can't comprehend and I don't have to, so!

Absolutions, solutions, I can see forth
To me I behold, the sun, the river I do not cross
But the grass between my toes and the earth
underneath my feet
I feel such comfort, grounded
Safe like under my duvet/sheet

I step beyond and look upon
And what I see I don't belong

Resolutions, absolutions, I still sing my song
And all I can say is Amen, gwaan and gwalong,
gwalong!

April 17th, 2013

ADULTS ONLY

Locking up, you know who that was now
And what she did, she sick
Lesbian, certainly don't receive no dick!

Disgusting parasite, attempting to fuck me up
But I should have learnt from the 'bird'
The first time she fucked me up

The sun shines bright, no longer dim
The wind blows strong and lowly sings

But I am not alone, even out in the cold
You see the older I get doesn't mean I get old!

Locking up whoever, no matter the wrong
Is probably quite simple, it's where they belong

You may forgive, even forget, but just don't fester on it
Locking it away was the right thing to do
Cos when you do a shit, you don't look at the pile, or
do you?

April 18th, 2013

<u>VOID</u>

Feeling of numbness
No quickening to awake
Just a voidness in that obtuse grey area
That trembles to wake

No occupancy, but eviction of thought
Nothing worthwhile observing to matter
No coin to flip, no matter how it falls, just emptiness
No problems to be sought

Why this emptiness, floating on thick ice
Not drowning, just lying there
Why doesn't it break?
Do I sink? Do I swim, I might not survive

Right now, not understanding these condescending
thoughts of mines
Normally flying like an eagle, soaring above through
the blue skies
Heavenly thoughts, far from mind, but I can express
the same of the other kind

I salvage my 'being', I look and stare into space
Seeing nothingness cos nothing is there
No clarity, no dimness, just extrapolatory thoughts
Nothing to vindicate this numbness of soughts!!!

Sx

April 20th, 2013

CUDDLES

If only he knew how much I appreciated him
Not just for his shopping, but for time loss not seeing
him

A cuddle, a kiss, is all a friend wants
To be held, pain taken for the moment
Lend released, exhale and knowing he's still there

You smile and then you smile some more
Is this life? Yes
Finally, I'm on the mend

Thanks for the cuddles, big hugs and the kiss
For that tiny little moment
You made my life Bliss!
Thank you

April 25th, 2013

MINES

Dog furs on my socks
Cat's fur black all over the kitchen floor
Fish swimming in dark water
Rabbits making noise in hutch

Just had to carry shopping on back
I might as well go to cafe than live in this badland

Man rubbish, something I knew from fifteen
Now big age tell me what's new

Still got dog fur on socks
Fish still swimming in dark water
Rabbits making noise
And man trying, attempting, big time to see me sinking

Drinking, not swimming, unless on own
So leave me with the dog fur on socks
Fish swimming in dark water
And rabbits making noise in hutch

Mines, I can deal with that, its' mines
You are something else, companion to a swine
I don't have one of those
And everything I do have is completely mines!

April 26th, 2013

<u>Too Long</u>

I need a bringer not a receiver
Why make me feel like I am begging
I believed, thought we were sharing

But now I understand you
And see the change in your manners
Missing you so badly
The way you treating me
It's so hard to continue and tired of waiting for change

When in my face it is the same
Fling back, I'm to blame
Consider the change, not in me
But you, the same
It's no secret we are the same

I need a bringer not a receiver
Someone who does, not a deceiver
All I see is blank
My feeling yet again sinking
I believe sank!

Where? What do I do?
Never, not now, I need someone forever
I'm not a shank, a tool, a lever
To that I can say, there's no me or you, NEVER!

April 30th, 2013

SOMETHING

What more can one say?
Words are power! Something said can be something
led
It depends on how you take it
Look around, see who's there
Take your hands in there's
And all they want to do is yours to share!

Well, it don't work like that
For me life, is hard; my health
Deteriorating and that's a fact!

What more can I say, but pray
Dear Father, Creator Most High
Has I look into the sky
Searching for His Most Divine, Unconditional Love

Hold me close, don't let me go
And wherever you take me I'll be there forever

See it had to get this far for me to realise
This gift and passion I have is endless
And hard to endure, to other I give
And what I give ain't useless
But something precious

So do wisely, I'll go beyond, invisible to you and everyone
One day, even now I am someone
So you overs me, I don't sit here on my hands

Waiting for my dues, my just deserts
If only I had that special someone to share it all with
But then I never feel like I failed
But in my faith I still prevail

My God, My Mother, I trust in them
Without their strength, I won't pretend
I wouldn't be here and then what then?
No more surrender, no more pretend

I'm not alone, to the world on my feet
My wibbly, wobbly legs, my broken toes
I do have something to show
Something I have learnt!

What have you got? Nothing!
Well guess what? I have something!
Health, strength, prosperity and wealth
That's not nothing, what more can I say?
Something!!!!!!!!!!!!

May 1st, 2013

LOOKING ON

I am yet but a shadow, a ghost
Amongst all those people, I ain't no spectre or a host

They walk around like robots waiting for any kind of
a reaction
I don't know for what they are reaching
To prompt them like the matrix or the cube that man
made them

Has sculptured them into nothing but just a slave
To be twisted, shaped and moulded until they match
All look the same
I'm not one of them. Them I do not blame
I observe what I see and feel quite alone
Immortal I'm not, but only in soul

I rise up my head and I pray as I touch
Just keep on reaching to feel that thing I long so much
At last it's there, I can nearly feel
The hands stretch out to me, I will HEAL!

May 5th, 2013

Spiritualism – Inner Self

My posture stands erect with my being
As my thoughts and imaginations transpose
Themselves to maximise into reality, what I am seeing

This Chakra, my karma, my spiritual self
Now interact, combine, as I become one with myself

I feel strong and healthy as I await my faith
Some call it my future, I call it my destiny
It's coming sooner than later, no more wait!

I blow, inhale, exhale, then relax
My eyes, behold an orifice, so lucid
Transparent, is that me I ask myself?

Oh yes I reply and you have been waiting a long time
But really it's only just been a while

No longer dormant, but ready to erupt
To seize and conquer, but not to corrupt

My life belongs to God and Mother Earth herself
I respect everything around me, as I do my own
health!

And when all comes to fruition and succeed I do
I'll praise my Father, the exalted one
I'll do as he commands me and all that he please!

May 29th, 2013

BIRTHDAY

Dear Father, Blessed Most High
Health, strength, wealth and prosperity
Please make my mother proud of me
And make her feel my spirit
As I pray to you right now for deliverance

I have worked so hard all my life
I seek reward, is that so bad?
I ask myself, not feeling sad but glad

I look upon people with a different face
Can't quite comprehend what I see
Or represent especially in a society, my place!

But Dear Father, Blessed Most High
As I burn my incense, inside I sigh
Quite tired but not quite burnt out
My books to promote, the show to prolong

Dear Father, Mother Earth, be proud of one
All I have ever wanted to be is succeed
So be proud, you have made someone!

In my books and my writing
My soul I express, on my face and my body language
I might seem depressed
But to show glory too soon I feel will do harm
The envy the ones, who feel they are charmed

I don't wish to take, but to make
I don't wish to eat all but to share with a break

Whatever My Father, unto you I pray
Cos I know my heavenly wishes
One day will come true

Sx

May 29th, 2013

CHILDREN

Our children, so young, excluded from school
For what, 'called a monkey', that's what they presume

Don't break him or melt him or manipulate him by smiles
Don't tell him you love him when you telling him lies

He's still naive but ambitious so much
Envy and jealously they reach out to touch

He holds out his hands not to realise
That the feel of their hands is filled with untruth
To break him and not reach a Man

But he will grow strong, tall and proud
Hold up his head and look upon
All those deceivers as they cry out his name
Please help our children, deliver them from intent and shame

Oh help our children, don't you remember my name
I was once your friend
Oh no not mines, to me you came, I was surprised

Fool me no more, go back where you belong
I am no longer that boy you held down, but nearly a
Man!

I woke up early, too early in fact
Looked out of my window, raining at that

Oh what a day, I have planned to do
My books to promote and some to sell too

My name is established, renowned in its way
Because existing, this lifestyle I don't want to stay

Oh rain, oh rain, please go away
A day I have planned and its gonna stay that way
Hooray

My son looks at me, I've got to help mummy today
I am going to help her in my own special way

June 14th, 2013

People

Don't go out of road
And let anyone slap you on the cheek
And turn your face so you can't speak

Don't put yourself in that position in the first place
Because you are the one that took up their space
Their word could be testimony to your fate
Because, trust me, you they hate!

Look at you now and look at them
Who is being punished, not me but truly them!!

June 24th, 2013

ILLNESS

Being ill for days now
Feeling like shelf can't speak or say how
Chest and lungs banging away
Shaking with fever
My tummy hurting, trembling all over

Turning around to find the right spot for comfort
Can't sleep cos everything, my joints hurt alot

I have to get out of bed
My feet are wobbling
My seeing is blurred, I rub them hobbling

Down the steps I descend into the kitchen
Where I remain and season my chicken
Not for me but my son to eat
I feel so hungry but feel defeat

Today I feel a little better
As I sit down and write a letter
My heart pours out and feeling sore
My skin it itches, as I perspire through pores

I take a bath to undo the way I feel
To take away this aching pain
Bye for now as I feel the strain
My body still aches and by writing this
I have nothing to gain!!!

July 1st, 2013

HAIR/WEAVE

An Angel came to on Friday
And suggested I get a make over
She then gave me her business card
That contained all of her information
To read, it wasn't that hard

I deliberated it, back and forth
And then on Saturday I gave her a call
The appointment I made 11am
The 1st of July, the first client to come

And guess the business name
As well as her own
Oh yes, Angel indeed
With the make-over/weave I need

And my hair looks fantastic
I feel anew and completely fresh
Thanks to Angel, I look my best!

Thanks Angel

August 5th, 2013

IT'S BEEN A LONG TIME

Imagination is a blessing
And reality a curse
You can be in a surreal calm state of body and mind
And then that someone comes around

Your life now becomes a reality
Your beliefs are secondary as they are primary
Their downfalls, yes downfalls
Fall on you like a waterfall

Washing you all over, but leaving you dirty, unclean
Tired, disabled, slow and incapable
They still stay around

It's tiring, this awakening
The impatience, they are like a shadow
You pray for your imagination
You dismiss the reality
For you its more comforting
For you it's ideal

It doesn't mean you just care about self
But self-preservation and an average of neutrality
To be calm and deal with all of the insanity

Imagination is what makes you smile
It takes you to depths that you knew exist
All of the while

For that I strive, I will survive
No longer an imagination, but actually my Life!

August 9th, 2013

PLASTERED

SX AND SON! To All my Beloved!

August 25th, 2013

SUNDAY

Oh my Lord, my light and my salvation
Who do I obey and hold in high esteem
You above all, My Creator Most High
My love, my undying attention to you I acclaim

Never leave my side, forever be my guide
And I will go willingly in your stead, as you lead
Me to higher ground

I praise thee, morning, noon and night
I feel you near me holding me tight
Never lonely, not even at night
Not afraid of the dark, as I stare at the moonlight

My God I pray unto thee
My faith, my body and spirit and soul
Belong to thee, Almighty one

Without you in my life I would be no one
Praise the Lord God, the Almighty one
I feel, I am so blessed, because of you I am someone!

September 7th, 2013

AWAKENINGS

I lift up my head banging out loud
Holding with both hands, afraid
I am here or within the Lord's shroud

God forgive me, I say aloud
Making my head hurt as I stumble about
My body it aches, I shudder with cold
Oh my Lord God, I feel so old

What earth possessed me?
To go to just rock bottom
What on earth suppressed me?
That I had forgotten

Oh Lord please forgive me, I truly pray unto thee
As I lift up my eyes crying
Thinking what could have possessed me
So that I had befallen unto thee!

I'm so blessed to be given this chance
Oh my Lord
And I hope to be strong always
With your love and support

Please don't leave me, I need you always
For you I can depend on
Don't lead me astray

Bless me Dear Father, keep me straight
Erect and forever in your arms for my sake

Forgive me my Father I hope I'm not too late
I'll go when you call me it's just myself I seem to hate

I must focus and rely on no one, only you are my family
Who makes me special and like someone

Bless me dear Lord and forgive me of all of my sins
And try to keep me straight and on the narrow
As I know you had planned

Thank you Father for all that you have done
For protecting us all, especially my son!!!

September 10th, 2013

VISIONS FOR NONE

Visions with no sight
How I sit here, in my plight
My bed I laid and I pay
The words to be said I cannot say

Visions with no sight
Through the darkness I see light
I try to run, can't somehow manage beyond
That hurdle within my sight

I crumble, I fall
I stumble, I drop
My legs are weakened, as I crawl
With a vengeance not to stop
I get up and stand tall

Visions with sight as I look into the light
My future still undetermined
For my ambitions I must fight

Visions with sight
My eyes they shine so bright
I look forward to my future
Every day and every night

I hold up my arm and look into the light
Visions for none, but I do see the end of my plight

I am not afraid of critical they are unto me
I am aware of danger, but more of what may lay
ahead for me

Face the visions with sight
And look upright
There is your future
Staring into your face
As broad as daylight

It's how you make it
Impossible or not
It's what pathway you walk
Just do not stop

Keep going don't run before you can walk
Cos that vision with no sight
Has now shown you the light!

September 28th, 2013

WHY ARE THEY SHOUTING AT ME AGAIN?

I wake up in the morn and stretch my body from
The curls of my sleep, my foetal position
I rub my eyes before opening them
I look around already determining my daily situation

Oh what has this day has in store for me
Is the sun shining? Lets' draw the curtains and see

Oh yes, this day will do, as I look into the morn
Looking at my neighbours doorways
So clean, pristine, not forlorn

But beauty and pride to share
With the world and a sight to behold
As they too awake to the chirping they hear

My day has began, my chores and routine
I move like 'I robot' that's just my life
I move on my own, my own player, no team

Nine out of ten calls I seem to get by
Some I ignore and pretend to be out
And then you get that someone
Who will yell and shout
For what I don't care or know about

All I can think about is why make this call at all
Why are you shouting at me again?
Go find someone else to call

I count to ten and exhale slowly
And then I pretend acting coldly
Not to hear or comprehend
The line is not working
"Hello, hello". I hang up
That's the end!

I look at the mobile and wait for the ring
I doesn't happen, I sigh, I sing
I look at the clock, just half hour to go
Then no more shouting to compromise
I can then relax and go on a downlow

I sit as I wait and wonder why or what?
Do they actually have a job
Or is that shouting at me makes their day
The f.....ing slobs!

Why are you shouting at me again?

September 29th, 2013

PEN

The pen just keeps on calling
'Pick me up, keep writing'
I, lying here as it's a beckoning
Please pick me up and with a little help
We'll keep writing

I'm your best friend, never keep me lonely
Together as partners I'm truly yours only

Not to be shared
Or compared
I'm your pen
Your right hand
Your memories, your thoughts I write
With your helping hand
This pen will write

Together as one
A work of art we can/will achieve
It is my business to make your work clear

Flowing, writing, drawing, sharing
Together as one, through me
Your pen will not stop working
Through me your pen will do the talking
Sharing your thoughts and hopefully not be boring

October 2nd, 2013

FACES FROM THE BLUE

I received a call from the past
My prayers answered, God heard them at last

A boy I met, a man come forward
Responsibilities, wife and child, do make it for me
quite awkward

He's here for a bit, but not to do shit
To inform me of all the good and things happened
In his life, basically, bullshit!

He misses his family so much indeed
And some money to raise for Christmas
Prezzies for people in need

To help and assist me and my child as well
The next two months should be quite swell

I thank the Lord and pray to him
For bringing me this friend, I pray to him

Thank you my Lord and all around
Cos no more fret, I'm homeward bound!!!

October 7th, 2013

Getting Kicked

Kicked in the face
Ah what a disgrace
How can this happen in my own place

Kicked two times
This don't go wid deh rhyme
But just to tell you this
It is the last time

Getting kicked in the face
Might just show me the case
That being on my own
In my own place
Finally I will be safe

You stay there and I stay here
Don't come near me and please beware

Cos kicked in the face
Will be there awaiting your return
Cos now stupid, you're in my place and it's your turn!!!

October 10th, 2013

OLD AGE

OMG, that's my age!
Turning out rhymes not like an apprentice
But an old sage

Still got waistline
Face intact
Can't remember though last time of sex attack!

OMG, go away,
Not my age
Not no sage

Taste it lingers, as what awaits
Just my wisdom for Jesus sake!

OMG, is this my age
Then is you can remember
Remind me of the old days. Lol!

October 10th, 2013

OLD AGE – CONT. PT2

Is this dementia
Or something I should remember

Tiredness, me ah mek same phone call twice
Doing things already done
Oh what a waste of time, sometimes thrice

Again is this dementia?
I don't want to remember?!

Too many questions to answer
And with all the doubt inside
Life is just an issue
Something I can't hide and besides who cares
About the issue!

Cos I don't!

So if this is dementia
Then I've got it without a doubt
I think I do things, NOT!
And then I SHOUT!!!!!!!!!

If this is dementia
And I truly hope not
Beseech me, cos alot of living to do
And plenty to catch up!!

October 22nd, 2013

MONDAYS

Monday, what can I say?
The rain is pouring
My house is warming
As I try to mellow out

I watch JK in morn and noon
And wait for the evening
To come, hope soon

So today may end
And tomorrow will come
And hopefully the week
Will be full of fun!!!

October 28th, 2013

MOBILES

You lose your head
You break a bone
Your back it hurts
You ring your phone

And no one answers
To hear your pain
And if they do
The reply is bland
The less to say plain

Your pain is nothing
You can control
You have your thing
That mobile phone

Those aches you dealt with
Have come to pass
Because to feel
It seems to last

You lose your head
To stress no less
Don't talk, no, response
No pity, no stress

They don't want to hear
So keep your pain to self to bear
But don't shelter within yourself
To feel that you have done your bit
When life's all done and you look on
You'll realise you done pure shit!

You want a mobile phone
Trust admit
It's the in thing to communicate
And verbalise, shit

To receive unwanted, phone calls
That you don't want to answer
So leave the Mobile phone alone
Your prayers, God will answer!

November 5th, 2013

A NEW ERA

YES MY DEAR, COURT AGAIN
HOW LIFE GOES AND HOW WE PRETEND
TODAY I KNOW, BECAUSE I'VE SEEN
THIS DAY, A NEW ERA SHOULD PROVE SUBLIME

IT WENT MY WAY, OF COURSE IT DID
THE JUDGE IN MY FAVOR, BECAUSE IT'S MY KID
IT ALWAYS DOES, COS IF IT DID NOT
THEN MAYBE A FIST THEY WOULD SEE
AND TO WIN WE WOULD NOT

NO SHIT, NO BULLSHIT
IT'S ALL DONE
A NEW ERA HAS JUS BEGAN

FOR ME YESTERDAY I MIGHT HAVE GOT 'BUN'
A NEW ERA COMMENCES, TO LIVE
SOLICITORS, JUDGES ARE ALL GONE, GONE,
GONE!

SOMEONE ELSE TO SUMMONS
HOPEFULLY, MAGISTRATES
NOT LIKE THE HIERACHY OF THE LORD OF
COMMONS!

November 9th, 2013

ME

Pressure gone; done resolution
Still no one but my babies
Found a solution – Me
Is my motivation
Self is my stimulation

Righteousness, my dedication
Being Me eventually
I will find the solution
Fulfilling my life in every situation

Father Most High Thanks
For this observation
And I'm thankful for your time-tap
In anticipation

Unaffected, now with no form of limitations
I see the light and forwardness
And with my might I'm unpretentious
To go forward in all walks of my life
And no longer to be negative
But positive in all my summations

November 10th, 2013

BEHAVIOURAL THERAPHY

I scream, I shout
I make nuff fuss
I break my rules, yes I cuss

I blow strong wind and make nuff noise
But only for attention in order to survive

If you paid me, mind me, you'd realise
That under stress I am, so toot to show
All my 'friends', I shun, I run

It's easier that way
It's the way I behave
To show my feelings
I don't to
I don't want to become no man's slave

Basically sorry for the way I am
But I am not going to change
I'm me, not a sham, GLAM!

November 20th, 2013

MAMA

No more beat down
Step up, buy a new gown
Too large to stay in yard
Too bright, to go outta sight
But be at large

Too good not to be strong
To profound not to prolong
To obsessive not to go on
Too aggressive to quit and sing good bye songs

True apologises never surrender
Till death do us part
This ain't no game 'ender'

December 2nd, 2013

MIND AH WONDERING

Today, I've got to harvest
Gather, reap, sow and glow
Rise in the sun and be blessed
No blemish here to show

Tomorrow I've got to go north
And then another direction
Some of sorts, west, maybe east
Who knows, south or back North at least

Somewhere, I've got to begin
Next week, I will begin again
To see another daylight
Another change, another sin

To feel the breeze
And feel the ease
When all the crap is burnt
I stand with a smile
And rap for a while
As monotony fills my life with ease

I have got to change with simple rules
My life has got to change
And to exist in this cruel world
I only have myself to blame!!!

December 30th, 2013

EATING UP SOUP IS LIKE
RACING WITH THE SUN!

Doing, done my Christmas
My daughter and my son
Tiredness all gone, I retire to bed
To sleep and dream of the rising sun

Christmas I plea, please come and go
We all know it is simply fun for show
But as long as the children receive their gifts
Then it is over and everyone goes

Now it's coming to an end
The dinner yet to come
Santa I aim to pretend
Resolution my power
No fault in procedure
As I aim to please

But this continuous action
To complete and hold onto my composure
Is proving such a strain
I literally can't wait for Christmas to go
And the New Year to come
With health, strength, prosperity
And alot more to gain

It's a New Year 2014
A New Year has just began
We commence with wishes and resolutions
And all to no end

But happiness spread and laughter infected
As everyone looks forward to this New Year
And all for the ever after

Happy New Year everyone
Blessed be to everyone! Sx

By Sandra Maddix and with the inspiration of her handsome young son Ceaké Maddix

These last few years have proven to prove that families can come together and become stronger even if everything in life goes against them; it just makes them STRONGER!

SX

Printed in the United States
By Bookmasters